Guarding Your Senses

By

Betsy Stowers Frazier

Guarding Your Senses
by Betsy Stowers Frazier

Printed in the United States of America

ISBN 978-1-60791-035-0

www.xulonpress.com

Guarding Your Senses

Forward

Many people dream dreams but few get to see their dream fulfilled. One of those "Dreamers," Betsy Frazier, came to my office one day in 2000 and shared a dream that she believed had been given to her by God. With the excitement of an expectant mother anticipating the birth of her child she described a ministry that she would develop to serve the poor and needy in Knox County. She painted a verbal portrait of a large building where food, clothing, and other necessary items would be shared with thousands of needy people. She spoke of a place of worship where the homeless and others would come to hear the gospel preached and taught and have their spiritual needs met. It was an elaborate dream that I knew would require a great deal of work and resources to fulfill. I listened to her and encouraged her and then prayed with her before she left my office to pursue her dream. Eight years later the dream that God gave birth to in Betsy's mind has become a reality, and as God often does, as that dream has taken shape He has revealed more of His dream to her.

Betsy is one of those unique people who not only hear the call of God and receive a dream from God but they also do their part and pursue that dream until God turns that dream into reality. I have had the privilege of being there when God's dream was being born in the heart of this woman. I have worked alongside a few of the hundreds of volunteers who worked with her to fulfill that dream, and I know thousands of people have been served and blessed by her dream.

I know as you read this book you will be challenged by this "Dreamer" to follow your own God-given dream. As she teaches you the importance of "***Guarding Your Senses***" she will also encourage you to step out in faith and dream a dream like hers that will serve others and glorify God.

Dr. Ronald Stewart
Senior Pastor
Grace Baptist Church
Knoxville, Tennessee

Introduction

"For I know the plans I have for you," says the Lord. "They are plans for good and not for disaster, to give you a future and a hope. In those days when you pray, I will listen. If you look for me in earnest, you will find me when you seek me" (Jeremiah 19:11-13 NIV).

Looking out the window in my home, I see a ground hog scrounging under the many autumn leaves in our flowerbed. His fur has thickened to prepare him for winter. At the same time, I see a squirrel on the other side of the yard, his mouth bulging with nuts. He scurries to bury his edible treasures in a special hiding place.

Just as God helps these animals prepare for the colder, leaner days ahead, He continually grooms each one of us too, in preparation of the inevitable upcoming days in our lives that will be trying and difficult. The squirrel's stash of nuts and the ground hog's thick coat show us how God takes care of the universe, takes time to provide for animals during the harsh winter months, will He not take care of us in our times of need as well?

We all remember good times in our lives when blessings seemed to be around every corner. We also recall dark days of despair when the cold winds of adversity blew hard and fierce.

Looking ahead in life, we all will face hard times again. Whether we crumble or stand strong will depend on one thing, and that is whether we allow God to groom us today so that He can prepare us for the days ahead. God's love and protection are there for the taking, just as the nuts ripen for the squirrels. God stands ready to encircle us with hope and courage and strength, to lift us when we fall. The key is to allow God to do his grooming. Too often we shut Him out or ignore Him during happy times, just when He needs to build us up for hard times to come – the same as when he thickens the groundhog's coat while the weather is still warm.

If you are ready to step into God's embrace, opening your heart more fully to Him in order to receive His gifts, there are four steps you can take today:

1. Study the Bible daily.
2. Memorize your favorite verses until they become a part of you.
3. Keep God's word alive in your heart.
4. Seek a personal relationship with Him daily.

Your spirituality is just like your physical body – you have to feed it if you want it to thrive. If you didn't eat any food for a whole week, how strong and healthy would your physical body be? Now think back to the last time you sat down and read the Bible. How can any of us expect to be strong spiritually if we aren't nourishing our souls with God's word every day?

You can overcome the problems and worries of this world. God has a special plan just for you and you alone, and He is continuously grooming you to become everything you were created to be. When you take the first step toward nourishing your spiritual self by reading the Bible daily – just as regularly as you feed your physical body with food – you will feel God at work in your life as never before. He will bless you, enlarge your territory, and give you the wisdom to handle the many blessings ahead.

The mission of this book is to help you fully receive these blessings from God. As you follow the four steps outlined above, the key to your success will be guarding your five senses of sight, hearing, taste, touch and smell from the ravages of this world. Your five senses face threatening dangers every day that can lead you down a path of peril if you are not on guard. They are the gateways to your soul. Nothing enters your mind or your body except through what you see, hear, taste, touch, or smell.

Each of your senses is a precious gift from God. With these gifts comes a responsibility to care for them correctly. To feel God's hand upon your life as never before, start guarding your senses today as if you were watching over pure gold, for your senses are more valuable than the finest treasures on earth. Your relationship with Jesus Christ, and guarding your five senses, is the key to your happiness, your hope, your fulfillment. Every time the door to one of your senses opens, be aware of what or who is entering. It is my prayer that after you read this book you will never again look at even the smallest incidents in life in the same way again.

May grace and peace be upon you.

In Christ,
Betsy Stowers Frazier

- A special thank you to Lisa McDonald who encouraged and helped me accomplish this God-ordained task.
- Appreciation and acknowledgment also goes to Lauren Mohundro for her exceptional artistic ability in the preparation of the artwork in this book.

- This book is dedicated to my 5 grandsons. To God be the glory

Chapter 1

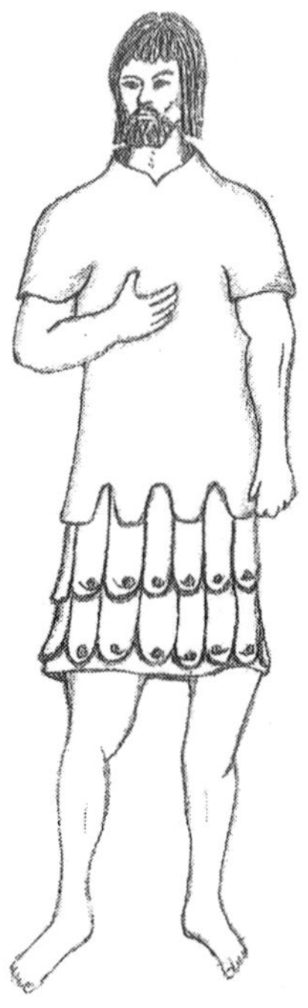

The Gateways to Your Soul

No matter what kind of home you live in, there is a doorway that leads inside. Whether you live in a big brick house in the suburbs, a college dorm, or even a homeless shelter or your car, the only way to enter your home is through a door. Some doors have strong locks and peepholes to see who is outside while others do not. But all doors have the same purpose: to keep intruders out and to keep those safe inside.

What could happen if you left your front door carelessly ajar? Rain could blow in, stray dogs could wander in, and thieves could prey on you. The unwanted visitors could put those inside the house in danger of all degrees.

Just as we have doors to our physical houses, we all have doors into our spiritual souls. These doorways are our five senses: sight, hearing, taste, touch, and smell. God has given us control over these doors. We are in charge of deciding when to open these doors and when to slam them shut. It is our choice.

In day-to-day life, we don't often stop to think about how important our five senses are. Every single moment of our lives, at least one of our senses is being used. Science tells us that in order to learn, we must tap into our senses. The more senses used in any given circumstance, the deeper the grooves are made in our brain and thus the stronger the memory. You could learn how a piano works by reading a technical book about it, but if you used more senses by hearing a concert pianist play a melody, touching the strings inside to feel the reverberations, and sounding out a simple tune on the keyboard with your own hands, you'd understand it even better.

Music is something dear to my heart, as I was a gospel singer earlier in my life. When a new song comes on the radio that I really like, first I hear it. The next thing I know, I'm using my sense of touch by keeping time with the beat by tapping my hand on my leg. Then all of a sudden I'm belting the song out, singing along. I visualize the lyrics, the words forming pictures in my mind. The words and the song become a part of me, often sub-consciously. The same goes for what you and I watch, listen to, talk about, read, or feel.

All of our senses are interconnected. The next time you order a pizza, notice what happens. First, you smell its tantalizing scent, and then you open the box and see all the juicy toppings and melted cheese. You take your first bite and taste the delicious blend of ingredients, and you hear the crust crunch. Later (especially if you eat too much) you even feel the fullness of our stomach.

Problems come when we open the door to one of our sense to something dangerous. Not just that one senses is affected; our whole bodies are.

As the Bible tells us, "For a good tree does not bear bad fruit, nor does a bad tree bear good fruit. For men do not gather figs from thorns; nor do they gather grapes from a bramble bush. A good man out of the good treasure of his heart brings forth good, and an evil man out of the evil treasure of his heart brings forth evil. For out of the abundance of the heart his mouth speaks" (Luke 6:43-45).

What God is telling us in this passage is that we will reap what we sow. If we put good things into our body, then we'll reap good things in life. It all comes down to what you and I allow to enter into our minds and bodies through the gateways of our five senses.

Think about the time you spend reading novels, magazines, and newspapers, and compare that to how much time you spend each day reading God's word in the Bible. God's word is there for the taking in the Bible. It inspires us when we are feeling down, it comforts us when we are at our saddest, and it can lead us out of deep valleys to new heights.

One summer when my daughters were young, they were helping at the country store that my husband and I operated. I had just received a large bill for dry goods, and I had no idea how we were going to pay it. Business had been slow, and we had very little money in our bank account. That morning before we opened the doors of the store, I read from the Bible and then led my girls in prayer, as I typically did at the start of our day. This time, though, I closed by saying, "Dear Lord, if it is your will for us to keep on running this store, please send us help today. Everything we do, we do for your honor and glory."

About two hours later, something happened that had never occurred before and never occurred again. A tour bus pulled up to the curb, and a crowd of out-of-town visitors came pouring into the store. In all the years we had run that little store out in the middle of nowhere, far from any big city, and in all the years my parents had ran the store before us, we had never had tour buses stop by. The sales we made that day covered the dry good bill, and then some, but more important than that was the impact the experience had on my daughters' faith in God.

If we want God there for us in bad times, we must read, study, and memorize His Word in the good times. If it is ingrained in us to turn to the Bible and to prayer, then we can fall back on Him in times of trouble. We can overcome life's most grueling hardships when God's words come to mind exactly when we need them most.

What type of music do you like to listen to? What kind of language do you hear when watching your favorite television shows? What are your conversations with your friends and family like? If you will take the following challenge for the next two weeks, I guarantee that it will change your life. For the next fourteen days, vow to yourself to listen only to good things. Expose your ears only to things that uplift you. Listen to spiritual music, watch TV shows that promote good morals, converse with people who speak well of others. Change the radio station if the music isn't spiritual, turn off the television if there are no wholesome shows on, and walk away if people are being unkind with their words, such as by gossiping. At the end of the two weeks, take a look at your life. You will be surprised at how your perspective and outlook on life have changed.

From the moment you wake up each morning until you go to sleep at night, your five senses affect your thoughts and shape who you are. As the Bible tells us in Romans 8:5, the mind of a sinful person is death, but one whose mind is controlled by the spirit has eternal life and peace.

You will be transformed by the renewing of your mind if you can break away from the patterns of this world. Resist conforming to what everyone else seems to be doing and saying. Listen to only those things that you know are right and good. This will allow you to test and approve what God's will is – His good, pleasing and perfect will (Romans 12:2).

Life is a choice. Every day, your life is a series of choices. God has made it quite clear that when we choose the spiritual over the physical it is like taking a giant leap toward God. Children often play a game called "Mother, May I." In the game, children are asked to take either small baby steps or giant leaps, and the winners are the ones who move ahead the fastest.

Sometimes when making choices, you may hear deep within yourself God telling you, "Yes! You are finally getting it!" Or you may feel that God is saying, "I wish she would listen to me more." You make choices every day that will affect you physically and spiritually. One way to make the right choices is to start putting everything into two categories: spiritual or physical. When you begin looking this way at your choices in life, it is as if a veil has been removed from your eyes. Because God is spiritual, we who worship Him must worship Him in spirit and in truth. We must make spiritual choices in life if we are to develop the spiritual side of ourselves. Every morning when you wake up and your feet hit the floor, you begin using your physical body the moment you wake up. But what about your spiritual side? How much do you exercise it? No wonder so many of us are weak spiritually. We are not exercising the most important thing in our lives – our spirit. Every one of us has 24 hours in a day. How much of those 24 hours do you spend exercising your physical body by walking, running, working out? How much exercise does your spirituality get by reading the Bible, praising God or praying?

You are a spirit on a human journey. In life, choose only those things that will help your spirit grow. Begin every day by spending time reading God's word. Pray, asking God to open your eyes to His word. Spend time talking with others about your faith and, just as importantly, listen to what God has to say back to you. The more you do this, the easier it becomes to recognize His voice.

We serve an awesome God, and He created us in His image. Yes, in the image of God *you* were created. So take charge of your life. Don't allow anyone to influence you to make bad choices. Remember it is your life, not theirs. You have the power to make the right choices.

When you make the decisions to choose spiritual things at every opportunity, you will be amazed at the way your eyes will be opened. God has so much in store for you. He is waiting to open up a new life to you. The first step is to open your eyes and be ready to receive His Word. You and I must openly search for His instruction.

When you have to make an important decision, sit down and list your choices. Step back and look for the ones with the strongest spiritual effect. Take control of every thought. Do not allow negative thoughts to be a part of you. Know that you are a child of God, that He will protect you better than any earthly parent could, and then relax. Once you commit yourself to putting God in control of your life, you can rest easy.

As the Bible tells us in II Corinthians 10:5: "Casting down imaginations, and every high thing that exalts itself against the knowledge of God, and bringing into captivity every thought to the obedience of Christ."

Here are some choices to begin thinking about today:

MUSIC: Will you choose something from the physical world such as country, rock, pop or rap, or will you listen to spiritual music? The good news is that today spiritual music comes in all types. Whether you like rap or country or pop music, religious singers perform spiritual songs with positive, uplifting lyrics in all styles of music.

CLOTHING: Are you wearing a low-cut, revealing outfit or something more modest and decent? The clothing we wear each day says a lot about us on the inside. The Bible says that your body, my body, everybody's body is a temple of the Holy Spirit. How will you choose to decorate your temple? Loosely or with care?

FOOD: In order to maintain your body, will you choose junk food or a healthy meal for breakfast? Will you allow alcohol and drugs to enter your body?

READING: Will you read murder mysteries, trashy love stories and horror novels, or will you read the Bible and books about Christian living?

TELEVISION: This is one of the strongest choices we can make because we are using two of our senses at once: sight and hearing. In what you are watching, is there foul language? Would the program be decent enough for you to sit down and watch it with Christ sitting down beside you?

TALKING: Gossiping is tempting for everyone. Are you going to join in and say malicious things about other people? Or will you be a peacemaker, changing the subject when someone makes an offensive comment about another person? When you were a child, did your mother or father say things that haunt you today? Will you be careful today not to make that mistake with your own children?

The Bible tells us, "Let no corrupt word proceed out of your mouth but what is good for necessary edification, that it may impart grace to the hearers" (Ephesians 4:29).

As you struggle to make the right choices today, also remember what the Bible says in I Corinthians 6:19:

"Therefore honor God with your body," and I Corinthians 3:16-17: "If anyone destroys God's temple, God will destroy him; for God's temple is sacred and you are that temple."

Do you ever get bored with your whole life? Life will never be boring to you again once you begin to walk with Jesus Christ. The scriptures assure us of this through King David's psalms: "How precious is Your loving-kindness, O God! Therefore the children of men put their trust under the shadow of Your wings. They are abundantly satisfied with the fullness of Your house and you give them drink from the river of Your pleasures. For with You is the fountain of life; in Your life we see light" (Psalm 35:7-9).

The disciple John wrote of Christ's purpose in his gospel: "The thief's purpose is to steal, kill, and destroy. My purpose is to give life in all its fullness" (John 10:10; NLT).

God promises us a better life. He will provide for us. He loves us with a love more powerful than we've ever received from even our family and friends. Most importantly, He offers us eternal life. What do we have to do to earn that? There is only one thing we must do: Trust in Him, not in the world. If we give up the worldly things that we've held dear and place our trust in God alone, our cup will runneth over in ways we could never have imagined. Our Heavenly Father, in His love, returns blessings to us more than our human brains can ever anticipate or understand. We will be living an abundant life.

As you begin to shut the doors of your senses to damaging situations, be sure to keep guard over the little things as well as the big. Satan needs only the smallest crack to weasel his way in.

A few years ago, my husband and I added a sunroom on to our house, which is way out in the country and surrounded by woods and fields. One day I opened the door to the sunroom, only to find a huge black snake coiled up right in the middle of the floor. I slammed the door shut and called my husband at work. He came home, and after searching the room finally found the snake in the closet and killed it. Longer than I am tall, the snake measured over six feet in length and was as thick as my wrist. We searched the house over and finally found the snake's entry hole – it was only about the size of an egg. He hadn't needed an open door to get in, only a small hole.

This holds true for our lives as well. Addictions and other harmful behaviors only need a toehold before taking over our lives.

Some people feel it is possible to flirt with the world's temptations without being affected. If you feel that way, I ask you to consider the following story.

A father was in the living room reading the newspaper when his two children came running into the room.

"Dad! Dad! Guess what?" they cried out.

Startled, the father dropped his newspaper and said, "What is it?"

"Dad, you know that movie we want to see? The one we keep telling you about? Well, it's at the mall theater, and we want to go. Can you take us?"

The father paused and then said, "What rating does it have?"

One of the children said, "I think PG-13. It's not bad, though. It only has that rating because of a few bad words and a little bit of violence. No nudity, I think."

"Well, does that make it okay?" the father asked. The children just looked at him not answering, shuffling their feet. "In my opinion, I don't believe you need to see it, but let me think about it. Hey, while I am thinking, would you like me to make my famous brownies for you?"

"Sure!" the children yelled and ran off into the other room.

About an hour later, the father called for them to come into the kitchen because the brownies were ready. Coming in, the children could smell the wonderful aroma, and their mouths started to water. They were excited and started to grab the brownies off the plate, but their father stopped them.

"Here are the brownies I promised you. I used about 90% all, pure ingredients, but there is just a small problem. I put in just a tiny bit of dog poop. But that shouldn't matter should it because 90% of the brownies are good, right?" The children quickly drew back their hands away from the plate and looked at their father with bewilderment.

He smiled a sly grin and said, "Now, what do you think we should do about that movie?"

Chapter 2

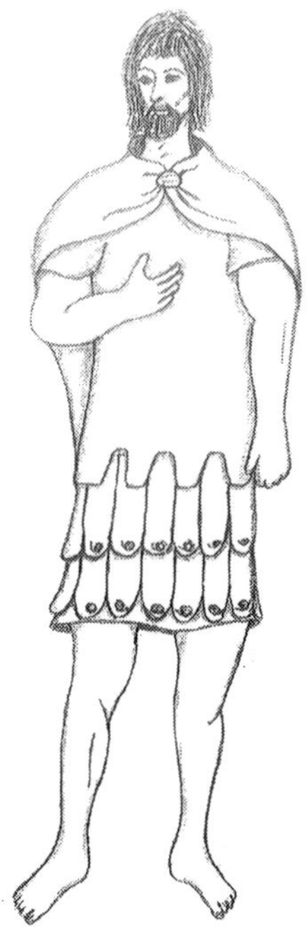

Your Body: The Temple of God

A friend of mine recently moved into a new house that was much bigger than her previous home. As she settled in, she told me of the joy she felt in finally having all the space she needed. Balanced against that, though, was the tough job of furnishing and decorating that spare bedroom, living room, extra bathrooms, and other nooks and crannies that she hadn't had in her last house. Faced with almost double the square footage of her last home, she began placing items in each room where they belonged. A bed here, a lamp over there, new purchases to make . . . three months later, she's still at work settling into her new home.

As she told me about her dilemmas and decisions while settling in her spacious new home, I thought to myself how our own bodies are just like my friend's house. Not only are we in charge of whom or what enters our doors, but we also have been given another important responsibility – caring for the rooms behind these doors.

I was reading my Bible a few days after visiting with my friend, when the following verse leapt out at me: "Now therefore you are no longer strangers and foreigners, but fellow citizens with the saints and members of the household of God, having been built on the foundation of the apostles and prophets, Jesus Christ Himself being the chief cornerstone, in whom the whole building being fitted together grows into a holy temple in the Lord, in whom you also are being built together for a dwelling place of God in the Spirit" (Ephesians 2:19-22).

This verse struck a chord in me because of the way it compares our bodies with a building whose cornerstone is "Jesus Christ Himself" and says that our bodies will be "a dwelling place of God."

In any church, there usually are rooms where people meet to study the Bible, a sanctuary containing pews, an altar, and a pulpit. With all the many parts of the church, the door is still the key. No one would be able to enjoy any of these rooms if they could not first enter the church through the door.

The Ephesians verse also describes our bodies as a "holy temple" and just as a temple or a church has a door, our physical bodies have the five senses serving as entrances. The various classrooms within a church could represent our mind: a place of training, learning, categorizing, sorting and researching. Pews located in the sanctuary could represent our will, a place where we sit, listen and yield ourselves to the molding and shaping due to the message we are listening to. The altar represents our heart, a place of confession and renewal. The pulpit, located at the front of the church, represents our desire, a place of evangelism, teaching and preaching.

Good things as well as bad things can enter through doorways. If sinful things enter through the doorway of our senses then there will be consequences: Our mind will be trained to be cynical, negative and morbid; our will then will be shaped by our thoughts; our heart will then be turned toward evil. We will then teach others what is in our heart. Like being addicted to a drug, we will be drawn more and more to the very thing which destroys us.

Some people who are allergic to a specific food find that they crave the food they are allergic to. Only after saying "no" again and again does this craving diminish. It is the same with the things of the world. We just say "no" over and over to reach the point where we see how good it feels to no longer crave the things that harm us.

As the Bible tells us in Matthew 12:33-35, "Either make the tree good and its fruit good, or else make the tree bad and its fruit bad; for a tree is known by its fruit. Brood of vipers! How can you, being evil, speak good things? For out of the heart the mouth speaks. A good man out of the good treasure of his heart brings forth good things, and an evil man out of the evil treasure brings forth evil things."

Let's look at alcoholic drinks for an example. If a person allows alcohol to enter his or her mouth, one of the five sensory doors, what would happen to the rooms inside that person?

MIND. The person would start to rationalize why he or she should be allowed to drink alcohol. "I need an escape because I am so stressed." "I deserve a break." "Only other people become alcoholics." "I can handle my liquor." "Just this one drink won't matter." "It's not too early for a drink."

WILL. With thoughts like those in mind, whenever this person sees a commercial for alcoholic beverages, a beer sign, or a bar, his or her willpower turns toward the alcohol instead of away from it.

HEART. Soon the person's whole life becomes focused on the purpose and goal of obtaining more alcohol. Alcohol becomes a trusted friend, and then it becomes his or her only friend. The person gives his or her life over to the short, fleeting thrill of the drink and the relaxing effect of its drug.

DESIRE. As a result, the person's whole purpose for living becomes centered on the pursuit of obtaining one more drink. Other things which were important before alcohol are now unimportant because of the strong hold the alcohol has on their system.

But what if this person opens the door to something positive? What if this person opens the door to Christ, the most powerful force that has ever existed?

The first step to opening the door is for the person to acknowledge that he or she is a sinner, as we all are, and to understand that none of us can save ourselves from sinful nature without the help of Jesus Christ. Then the person must ask Christ Jesus to enter his or her heart as Lord, Savior, Master, and King of their life. With that simple but powerful act, the person has opened a doorway that will lead to a whole new life. What happens to the rooms in the person's body?

MIND. The person will begin to learn more and more about God and the Messiah, Jesus. This will transform the way he or she thinks, and thus how he or she acts and lives life. As the Bible tells us, "Therefore, you will fully know them by their fruits" (Matthew 7:20 AMP).

WILL. The person will begin to conform his or her will to what the Holy Spirit directs them to do. It will begin to be easier to listen to the "still small voice" inside, which is the Holy Spirit directing a path. There will be an inner sense of wanting to do what is right.

HEART. The heart will be humbled and amazed as the person realizes that God knows all of the person's sinful behavior and loves him or her anyway. This love will spill over and cause the person to love others and will develop into a drive to do what is approved in the sight of God.

DESIRE. This person will have a strong urge to share the good news of Christ with other people because of the transformation of his or her life. He or she will feel a strong desire to help other people, putting personal desires and wants to the side. The person will want to read the Bible, spend more time in prayer, and more time listening, so that a relationship with Jesus Christ grows and develops until He is truly the person's best friend. (Where is the fruit in our life?)

At the start of every day, each of us must ask, "What is my desire? What is most important to me?" Our good friend Webster's dictionary describes "desire" as "to wish or long for, crave or to have a yearning." It is critical for you and me to know our heart's desires, because we will open our doors to whatever it is that we truly desire.

What is the solution for the times when we have bad desires? Jesus told us this Himself when He gave the Sermon on the Mount: "But seek first the kingdom of God and His righteousness and all these things shall be added to you" (Matthew 6:33).

When the verse says "these things," what was He talking about? Let's see what He said earlier in this scripture: "Therefore, do not worry, saying 'What shall we eat?' or 'What shall we drink?' or 'What shall we wear?' For after all these things the Gentiles seek. For your heavenly Father knows that you need all these things" (Matthew 6:31-32).

So, since our Heavenly Father knows our basic needs (food, drink, clothing, etc.), He told us what our desires should be first and foremost. We are to seek first His kingdom, which means to seek first God's way of doing things and God's way of thinking about things. If we will trust in Him and do this, our needs will be met.

The closer we get to God, seeking more of Him in an intimate relationship, we will know Him better and more of our desires will come into line with what He would have for us.

Having said all this, let's poise a few questions: If our bodies are the temple of God, how sturdy is God's house? How sturdy are the doors? Are the rooms clean of clutter? We are the guardians of our bodies, which make up God's temple. We decide whether to open our doors or not.

I knew of a man who had lived next door to the same neighbor for many years without ever taking the time to speak to him. Even when passing by this neighbor on the way to the mailbox, he never bothered to stop and chat. They lived side by side for more than 25 years without saying hardly a word to one another. Then the man began having major heart problems. It seemed that the doctors felt there was not much left to do for him. As a last resort they were going to try a heart transplant. But the man's heart was in such poor condition that none of the doctor's wanted to touch him. However, there was one specialist in town who might do the transplant. If only they could reach him before it was too late.

There were problems getting the doctor to consider performing the operation. After exhausting all efforts to get in to see the doctor, the ill man decided to look up the doctor's residential address and catch him at home and plead for his help. When the man found the address, he saw that to his amazement the doctor was his neighbor – the man who lived next door. The man had lived right beside the doctor all the time.

Do you need a heart transplant of sorts? Do you need a fresh start on life? How many times have you passed by Christ, ignoring Him, being too busy to speak or listen? He stands by, waiting for you to call out to Him. Let's begin the journey with Him today.

Chapter 3

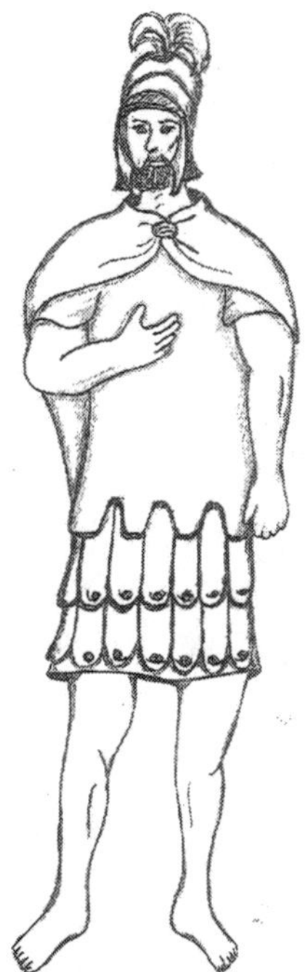

What's That In Your Eye?

"The lamp of the body is the eye. Therefore, when your eye is good, your whole body also is full of light. But when your eye is bad, your body also is full of darkness" (Luke 11:34-36).

How many times have you driven somewhere, perhaps to work or to a favorite shopping mall, only to realize after reaching your destination that you don't remember driving the last few miles? At times like that, it seems as if the car drove itself. But, if someone asked you to describe a wreck that you had passed by on that drive, you most likely could describe the wreck in great detail. Why could you recall the wreck but not the mundane road signs and traffic lights that you passed? It's because the wreck, being something tragic and different from normal, was more interesting and caught your attention. Your mind directed your eyes and your attention to the wreck.

It is up to us to decide where we look. From the moment we open our eyes in the morning, many things are before us. Our brains tell our eyes in which direction to focus. We can gaze at the good or the bad, opening wide the door of our eyesight. What we look upon could direct our whole life and also affect everyone we come in contact with.

Think about specific ways we use our eyesight. When we glance at something, we look quickly and briefly. When we gaze, we look earnestly, staring intently.

In the driving scenario above, viewing the wreck could be described as a "gaze." Because a car wreck differs tragically from the ordinary, it catches our attention. In comparison, we sometimes barely glance at road signs because we're already so familiar with them.

Your sense of sight is used continually during your waking hours. Millions of images are sent through your retinas and then to your brain through the optic nerve. Your brain then explains what the images are. In order to guard the door to your sense of sight, you have to make millions of decisions a day whether to glance briefly or to gaze intently.

If you watch television or open a magazine today, you will see how sex is used for advertisement. It is difficult not to come across the many commercials and programs that bombard us today, but each of us can make a decision as to whether to look more deeply or to turn away. We all have the opportunity to turn the television off or change the channel if we wish. If someone succumbs to the enticement and begins to stare at this type of programming on a regular basis, he or she may not be satisfied with obtaining soft-porn and may eventually move up to hard-core pornography. A person who frequently looks at pornography will likely become desensitized to love. His or her ideas regarding lovemaking will become warped.

If the person instead makes the decision to focus his or her vision on honorable things, such as family members, moral television shows, the Bible, the wonder of nature in the outdoors, and other wholesome things, then that person's life becomes more worthwhile. Every aspect of the person's life is strengthened because all of our actions are a direct result of where we have directed our sight.

To coin a phrase from a local Christian bookstore, "What goes in a heart comes out in a life." If the eyes are the windows to our soul, the soul is where our emotions lay. The ancient Hebrew and Greek writers felt that the heart was the center of a person. So then what we look at will affect all areas of our life.

A year ago, a young woman startled me when she shared her testimony with me. By opening the doorway of her sight to horror movies, her entire life became driven by a negative force that drove many dear people in her life away from her. It began in her teens, when she became a fan of scary movies, the gorier the better. She began reading horror books and searched out monster magazines. Soon, her whole life was focused on the venues associated with horror. It became her purpose for living. She was so persistent in her efforts that she would make a two-hour round trip to her sister's apartment 50 miles away just to see the newest horror movies on cable since she didn't have cable in her home. On dates, she would drag her boyfriends to these movies even when they said they'd rather see action movies, or drama, or even love stories – anything but another horror movie.

As she became consumed with the whole idea of mystery, suspense, and monsters, she became fascinated with the occult. She used an Ouija board in an attempt to talk to spirits. As her appetite grew, she fed it more and more. It got to the point where gore did not affect her – she didn't bat an eye at seeing heads split open with axes or people being disemboweled with a meat hook. She could sigh through any one of the movies with a straight face and say, "Is that it?" During this time, her sister asked her why she was becoming so morbid.

Thankfully, her Heavenly Father brought her out of this obsession. God showed her that fear had become a stronghold in her life because she had fed it with all the horror paraphernalia for such a long time. By watching so many of these movies and reading all the horror books she could find, she had opened the door for fear to not just walk but run right in. Her sense of sight was the first door it entered, but by the end it affected her whole personality, her actions, the way she thought about things, her relationships with other people and ultimately, her whole concept of life.

God's grace is sufficient and through His grace this young woman today has come out of this obsession. She says she still battles the worry and fear that overcame her after she became addicted to all the evil things she became associated with, but she understands that that is the cross she bears for the poor decisions she made in the past. Just as an alcoholic can possibly never walk into a bar without craving that next drink, she still occasionally craves watching a horror movie, especially when she sees an advertisement for a movie she saw in the past or watches a psychic network commercial. As this young woman's story tells us, the eyes are definitely the windows of the soul. What we focus our eyes on will shape our souls, our personality, who we are, and how we relate to other people.

As you struggle to keep yourself pure and holy, begin by making decisions about what you will focus your eyes upon. Don't sit passively when something comes before your vision. There is no innocent diversion. Satan is trying to take you over, to kill your spirit, your body, and your witness.

Keep in mind that we don't always see sin for what it is: there isn't a neon sign flashing a warning. Satan doesn't need a wide-open door; he only needs a crack to worm his way in, and believe me, I speak from experience unfortunately. When I was in my early 40s, I became unhappy in my marriage. My husband and I seemed to be going out of our way to make each other jealous, and our relationship seemed to be falling apart to the point where I was actually considering divorce, something I wanted to avert if all possible. Being religious, I knew that I should turn to God for strength, and I normally would never have considered calling a psychic hotline, having my fortune told, or anything like that. And Satan knew that. But a woman I knew through work had great faith in psychics, and she had an upcoming appointment with a famous psychic who had a six-month waiting list. The day of the appointment, an emergency came up. Knowing that there was no way she could keep her appointment, she offered it to me. I am still ashamed to this day that I took it, with great hopes that the psychics would have answers for me about my marriage. Needless to say, I found the encounter to be an empty sham, ending with a thinly veiled sales pitch for more ways for me to waste my money. In the end, my marriage was saved, but the psychic had nothing to do with it. My marriage turned around only after I put God back in the center of my life instead of off to the side where I had pushed Him. It was ironic: During the years I had made my husband "my god" and was living my life trying to please him, our marriage began to fail. When I put God back at the forefront of my life, my marriage turned the corner and began to thrive again.

I am just so thankful that during the period of turmoil in my marriage that I did not become addicted to the promises of psychics, which I am sure, is a strong allure for some. I am so sorry I hurt My Heavenly Father, but praise God I serve a forgiving God, and when I asked His forgiveness He graciously forgave me and our relationship was restored.

The Bible tells us, "So I say live by the Spirit and you will not gratify the desires of the sinful nature. For the sinful nature desires what is contrary to the spirit and the spirit what is contrary to the sinful nature. They are in conflict with each other so that you do not do what you want" (Galatians 5:16-17).

All of us have it within us to bond with God and break the spell of hurtful addictions. One woman I know continues to struggle terribly; she doesn't yet realize that the simple act of closing her doorways to temptation would turn her life around.

When it all began, it seemed innocent to her and her family. As a teenager, she began reading *True Romance* Magazine. Next she began reading short paperback romance novels and then longer hardback versions. Before she realized what was happening, she was reading several of these books a day. Her life centered on these romance tales that absorbed her, creating an unrealistic ideal in her mind. She became more and more unhappy with her husband, her looks, her home, her whole life. Today she is in agony because she feels that nothing in her life is as perfect and exciting as that of the fictional characters in these romance novels. She is one of the most miserable people I have ever known.

Satan begins with small steps, every time. He looks for the tiniest crack to enter. The first step is so subtle that you hardly recognize what is happening or who is doing it.

Today, make it a point to actively monitor what you let your eyes rest on. Pay special attention to the routine things in your life. What do you see that makes you feel wholesome and good about yourself? What detracts from the person you want to be? Figure out a way to let your eyes light on the good more often, and a way to dim the lights on the bad.

Chapter 4

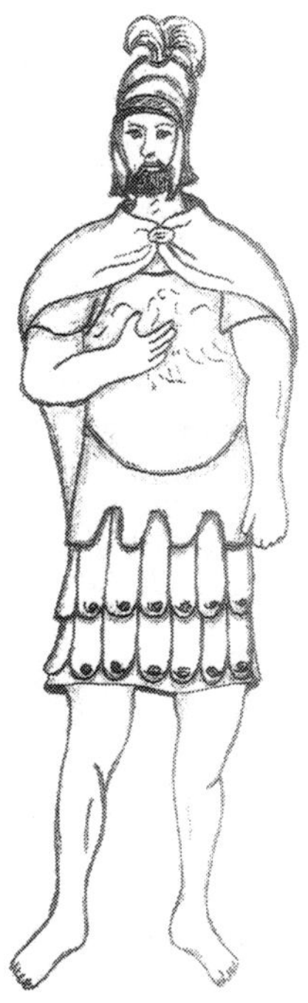

Our Sense of Smell

Shaped like a warped triangle from a bit of cartilage, your nose is another vital gateway into your body.

Leonardo da Vinci believed that the nose set the character for the whole face, and the story of Genesis in the Bible shows how important this part of our anatomy is to God. As the Bible tells us in Genesis 2:7, "And the Lord formed man of the dust of the ground, and breathed into his nostrils the breath of life; and man became a living being."

It is through the nose that the air enters the body – bringing life-supporting oxygen. And it is through the nose that we breathe in all kinds of scents.

Like all of our senses, what we allow to come in through the doorway of the sense of smell can have a powerful impact on our whole body. Think of cigarette smoke – clinical studies have shown that even breathing second-hand smoke from someone else's cigarette can have harmful effects on your lungs. Cigarette smoke even causes more wrinkles in our skin, affects the color of your hair, damages vocal chords and discolors fingernails and teeth.

In today's world, one of the main ways in which we must guard our sense of smell involves drug use.

This often begins in high school when teenagers sniff glue, aerosol cans, or other toxins in order to obtain a temporary "high." This can be the first step down the slippery slope to hard-core drug abuse in which a person's life is turned upside down.

One blond-headed young woman, who had grown up in a loving, middle-class family who tried to give her every opportunity, told of how trying drugs "just one time" had taken her down into a deep, dark valley that she didn't think she'd ever be able to climb out. A handsome boy she had a crush on offered the drug to her, and she thought she could try it just one time to see what it was like. Instead, she became addicted immediately. Soon she was living only for her next chance to get hold of the drug again.

She lost everything – not jut her physical possessions but even her family and friends as she found herself willing to do anything necessary in order to get drugs, including stealing from them and others. She ended up in jail – again and again.

After years of living this way, she began to hate her life and hate the person whom she had become, but she still could not give up drugs because of the power they held over her. She felt ashamed of what she had become, so ashamed that she couldn't stand to look in a mirror at her reflection.

Then one day when she was back in a jail cell again, someone handed a Bible to her. As a child, she had been raised by a Christian family that went to church regularly, and there had always been a Bible lying around her house. But this time when she opened the Bible, it was different. She began reading its pages in earnest.

A verse jumped out at her: "If you devote your heart to him and stretch out your hands to him, if you put away the sin that is in your hand and allow no evil to dwell in your tent, then you will lift up your face without shame. You will stand firm and without fear" (Job 11:13-15). Reading that verse, she found her face wet with tears. What she wanted more than anything was to be able to hold her head up without feeling shame, and she realized that the key was through God.

She kept on reading, and for the first time in her life really understood the gift that God gave to all people through Jesus Christ.

Once she realized that God loved her, and that through His love she had the greatest power in the universe on her side, she felt strong enough to stand up to the terrible hold that drugs held over her. Three years later, she remains drug-free and is a devoted Christian. She says that she is happy and fulfilled for the first time in her life.

Still, she looks back with terrible regret over the lost years of her life – more than a decade of her life was lost, wasted during the time she was addicted to drugs. Tears still spring to her eyes when she thinks of how she hurt her mother and father during those terrible years. By giving in "just one time" to the temptation to misuse her sense of smell and breathing in a drug, she lost years of her life that she can never recover, and she hurt people in ways she will never forget. They have forgiven her; God has forgiven her. She has even forgiven herself. But still, the memories remain.

Chapter 5

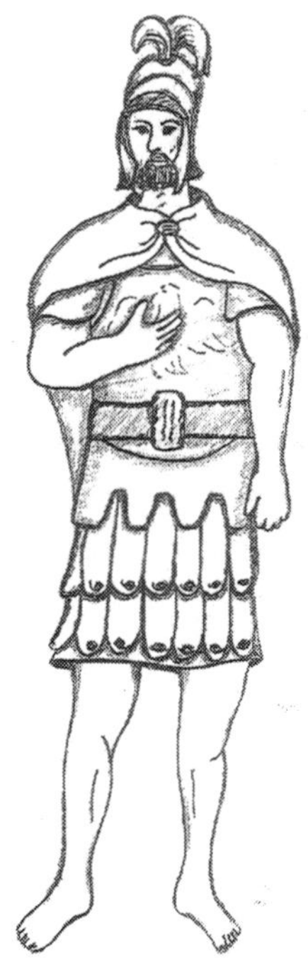

Do You Hear What I Hear?

Imagine yourself in John's position when he was viewing the things of heaven as he wrote the Bible's book of Revelation. He was swept away in the spirit to the throne room of heaven where he heard four creatures there worshipping:

"The four living creatures, each having six wings, were full of eyes around and within. They do not rest day or night, saying "Holy, holy, holy, Lord God Almighty, Who was and is and is to come!" (Revelation 4:8-9).

John wrote: "Then I looked, and I heard the voice of many angels around the throne, the living creatures and the elders; and the number of them was ten thousand times ten thousand, and thousands and thousands, saying with a loud voice: 'Worthy is the Lamb who was slain to receive power and riches and wisdom, and strength and honor and glory and blessing!"

"And every creature which is in heaven and on the earth and under the earth and such as are in the sea, and all that are in them, I heard saying, 'Blessing and honor and glory and power be to Him who sits on the throne, and to the Lamb, forever and ever!" (Revelation 5:1).

Can you imagine being in John's shoes and hearing this with your own ears? How would each of us be changed if we listened to God's word as much as we currently listen to the negative messages on the airwaves and in conversations around us in the world today?

Our lives would drastically be changed if we, as a people, would protect our sense of hearing and carefully guard what we let in. Our senses are interrelated – what enters by one sense will affect all the others. What we hear with one sense will affect all the others. What we hear with our ears affects what we think and say and, ultimately, what we feel in our hearts.

If we know that listening to the things of God is better for us, then why don't we do it? It is because all humans are born with a sinful nature. Unless we put ourselves under the Holy Spirit's control, our flesh will respond to the temptations of this world, which is almost always contrary to what God is calling us to do.

Not wanting to listen to God is not something new that happened just in this generation. Remember the exodus out of Egypt with Moses and the Israelites? Moses had been on Mt. Sinai receiving the Ten Commandments and other laws which the people were to follow. God told Moses: "Behold, I come to you in the thick cloud that the people may hear when I speak with you, and believe you forever" (Exodus 19:9).

God's purpose was to establish an intimate relationship with His people, just as He wishes to establish a personal relationship with you, right now, just as you are.

The people responded: "All that the Lord has spoken we will do" (Exodus 19:8).

Moses prepared the people with a cleansing process and specified regulations about how close they could come to the mountain because it was a holy place, a place where God dwelled. The time for God to speak came after Moses delivered the Ten Commandments.

"Now all the people witnessed the thunderings, the lighting flashes, the sound of the trumpet and the mountain smoking and when the people saw it, they trembled and stood afar off. Then they said to Moses; 'You speak with us, and we will hear; but let not God speak with us, lest we die'" (Exodus 20:18-19).

God had rescued them from Egypt and their slavery. The people had seen miracle upon miracle: the manna from heaven, the water from the rock, the bitter waters made sweet. So the issue wasn't that they did not know what God had done for them. He was their deliverer and provider. And all He wanted to do was commune with them. But they were afraid and said they still wanted Moses to be a mediator between God and them.

Someway, somehow, in order to fully experience the glory God has set aside for us and to walk under the Holy Spirit's direction, the human race must learn how to listen and to filter what we hear. How do we train our flesh to hear only those pleasing things and to heed the directives of God?

The Bible says, "I urge you therefore, brethren, by the mercies of God, to present your bodies a living and holy sacrifice, well-pleasing to God, which is your spiritual service of worship" (Romans 12:1).

In I Peter 2:5, this same theme is echoed: "You also, as living stones, are being built up a spiritual house, a holy priesthood, to offer up spiritual sacrifices acceptable to God through Christ Jesus" (1 Peter 2:5).

To "sacrifice" means to give something up. In the Old Testament, a sacrifice was symbolized by the death of an animal. These offerings resulted in the death of a certain type of animal, depending on the sin. In order for us to be that holy priesthood and the spiritual house that Peter speaks about, we must "sacrifice" our flesh, our ears included, to God. By "sacrifice," I mean that we must give up our own selfish desires and let them go. A well-known speaker once said, "Christians understand the concept of offering themselves as a sacrifice. The problem is that the verse says we have to be a *living sacrifice*. The fire gets hot on the altar so we keep jumping off."

What the speaker was saying was that it is hard to be a living sacrifice because that means resisting the daily temptations that come our way. Yet, as you will discover, the more you practice living a holy life, the more natural it will become to you and the better you will feel.

Today in the United States, most homes have at least one Bible, if not several, and in Christian homes there typically are several books written about the bible on the bookshelves. We don't know how lucky we are to be able to pick up a book and read God's word anytime we want. This was not the case in Biblical times, when books of all types were extremely scarce. The making of each Bible required the skins of several animals, and the scriptures had to be handwritten by scribes – a very laborious and expensive process. The majority of the people did not have personal copies of the Word to refer to at a moment's notice. The only way they could learn the ways of God was to hear a priest or other official read the Bible to them.

"Now the king sent them to gather all the elders of Judah and Jerusalem to him. The king went up to the house of the Lord with all the men of Judah and with him all the inhabitants of Jerusalem – the priest and the prophets and all the people, both small and great. He read in their presence all the words of the Book of the Covenant which had been found in the house of the Lord. Then the king stood by a pillar and made a covenant before the Lord, to follow the Lord and to keep His commandments and His testimonies and His statutes, with all his heart and all his soul, to perform the words of his covenant that were written in the book. All the people took a stand for the covenant" (II Kings 12:1-3).

Moses commanded that the entirety of the law be read to everyone in Israel every seven years (Deut. 31:9-13). Every man, woman and child living in Israel was to hear the entire Word of God every seven years. In between, they would hear bits and pieces of the Word being read by the priests during feasts and celebrations.

In this age, when we can read God's word for ourselves by reading the Bible over the Internet or by buying an inexpensive copy from nearly any shopping mall, we still need to *hear* God's word on a frequent basis – not just read it. One of the best ways to do this is by attending a weekly church service.

By joining a church and attending regularly, you receive many blessings:

- You have a pastor, a spiritual leader, whom you can turn to for religious guidance and for an interpretation of passages in the Bible that puzzle or intrigue you.
- You gain the friendship and support of other church members who are there for you in times of need.
- Your spirituality and commitment to the Lord is routinely refreshed by hearing God's word at weekly services.

Make a vow today to make changes regarding your sense of hearing. Don't listen to music that has negative lyrics. Avoid being a part of conversations that are unkind, such as gossiping, and see if you can make it through a day without criticizing anyone (including, and especially, your children.) Turn off television shows that promote immoral lifestyles. Don't hang around people who use profanity, who put down others, or who verbally abuse you.

Replace all these negative things with sounds and conversations that make you feel good. Find a radio station that plays uplifting music with a spiritual message. Form friendships with people who are positive and encouraging. Be upbeat with your own words – as the late author Alex Haley said, "Find the good and praise it."

Chapter 6

What Did You Say?

I will never forget the anguish I saw in the eyes of two children during a quiet incident that occurred one day when I was volunteering at the charity Angelic Ministries in downtown Knoxville, Tennessee.

A mother in her 30s had come to us for clothing for herself, her nine-year-old daughter, and her 14-year-old son. As I do with all those who come through our doors, I began talking with her, trying to build a relationship with her as we searched for clothes that fit the three of them. The goal of our organization is to fill people's spiritual needs as we fill their physical needs for clothing, food, and shelter.

After a while, the mother opened up to me. She told of her desperation to get out of her homeless situation and of her involvement with a boyfriend who felt that her children were a nuisance and a bother. With her children standing there listening to every word of our conversation, the mother told me that her boyfriend had asked her to move into his house with him, but with one condition: she had to get rid of her children first. She asked if I knew of anyone who might take in her children for a couple of months, or even a year or two.

Near tears, the daughter spoke up, pleading with her mother not to leave them.

"Mom, please, we'll do anything. We can make it if we stay together."

The mother pursed her lips and shook her head, saying that she wanted to live somewhere other than the homeless shelter and that she needed some time to herself to search for a job.

The hurt I saw in these children's wide eyes as their mother off-handedly made these comments will likely haunt them for the rest of their lives.

Many times we don't realize the harm that can be done with mere words. We know that if we hit someone with our fist it will hurt them, but we often don't stop to think of the sting that our words leave. I wish that every mother and father could stand in my shoes at Angelic Ministries and hear over and over as one adult after another shares tragic stories of how words from a parent during childhood haunts them still.

I've met many homeless adults who are deeply convinced that they are worthless because their mother and father told them so repeatedly when they were young children.

We forget how much power is in our words. Our words from our mouths can be a gift or a curse. I pray that from this day forward you will be ever mindful of just how important every word that comes out of your mouth really is. You can build someone up or tear them down. It's your choice!

Another incident I've never forgotten occurred in the winter of February 1959 when three rock-and-roll musicians decided to take a plane to the next city on their concert tour. Buddy Holly, the Big Bopper, and Rudy Valens were traveling by bus when, due to the harsh winter weather, their bus broke down. A plane was chartered to get them to their next destination on time. There was not enough room on the small plane for everyone, so Rudy Valens traded places with one of the band members, Waylon Jennings, after flipping a coin. In jest while getting on the plane, Buddy Holly yelled at Waylon Jennings, "I hope the bus breaks down!" Jennings joked back in reply, "Well, I hope your plan crashes!" The plane did crash and all aboard were killed.

Can you imagine how Waylon Jennings felt after hearing of the crash! Of course what he said did not cause the crash, but he felt terrible. He couldn't undo the words he had said.

Many of us have been in the same predicament. We can all think back to words we wished we hadn't said because they hurt someone. Everyday we are in situations that force us to make a choice between saying something good and edifying to someone or saying something critical and judgmental. All of us can remember the chant we learned while growing up: "Sticks and stones may break my bones, but words will never hurt me." Yet sometimes it is the harsh words that hurt us far more than physical blows.

God tells us in His Word that we will be held accountable for every idle word we speak: "For by your words you will be justified, and by your words you will be condemned" (Matthew 12:37).

With most of our senses, we must guard what comes in. When it comes to the mouth, we not only have to guard what comes in through our sense of taste, but also what comes out of our mouths through our speech. In Ephesians 4:29, the Bible tells us, "Do not let any unwholesome talk come out of your mouths – but only what is helpful for building others up."

In another chapter, Job says, "I am unworthy...I put my hand over my mouth" (Job 40:4). It would be easy to prevent saying the wrong things by just closing our mouths, staying mute, and not speaking a word. But this is not practical and also goes against what Jesus gave to us as the Great Commission. We are to be evangelistic and share his words and to make disciples of people in the world. We cannot do this if we are not willing to communicate.

Our culture today is very impersonal. Answering machines take messages for us if we do not want to speak to the person on the telephone. Food can be ordered from a faceless machine in the drive-through lane of a fast-food restaurant. Computers can be used to communicate with people all over the world via e-mail without seeing their faces. All these person-less avenues we have in our communication have created a major problem. People most of the time say the wrong thing because, as a group, we are unable or unwilling to get to know the other person we are speaking to. The more impersonal we are, the easier it is to say the wrong things. If I am not willing to walk a day in your shoes, how can I possibly understand your trials and give you encouragement or advice?

Even if we spend the time getting to know the people we come in contact with every day, how are we supposed to speak? Where do we go to learn how to control our speech and use it only to build people up instead of tearing them down?

Here is an experiment you can try. For one day, dress like a homeless person and go shopping. Will you be treated differently? How will people speak to you?

The Bible I use has chapter headings in each book. The heading from Chapter 3 in the book of James is "The Untamable Tongue," which tell us, "Look also at ships; although they are so large and are driven by fierce winds, they are turned by a very small rudder whenever the pilot desires.

Even so the tongue is a little member and boasts of great things. See how great a forest a little fire kindles! And the tongue is a fire, a world of iniquity. The tongue is so set among our members that it defiles the whole body, and sets on fire the course of nature, and it is set on fire by hell.

"For every kind of beast and bird, or reptile and creature of the sea is tamed and has been tamed by mankind. But no man can tame the tongue. It is an unruly evil, full of deadly poison.

"With it we bless our God and Father and with it we curse men who have been made in the similitude of God. Out of the same mouth proceed blessings and cursing. My brethren these things ought not to be so. Does a spring send forth fresh water and bitter from the same opening? Can a fig tree, my brethren, bear olives or a grapevine bear figs? Thus no spring yields both salt water and fresh" (James 3:2-13).

These verses show us how important it is to control our tongue. For such a small part of our body, it exerts a lot of power. It is a paradox. With it we can encourage others or we can curse them - it is our choice.

Let me share with you a dream I had several years ago after my mother passed away at the early age of 68. In the dream, she and I were walking down a pier with lots of ships. One stood out from the rest because of its gleaming beauty. The hard wood floor was freshly polished, the side walls painted snow white, and the hand rail shiny, newly refinished.

As my mother and I strolled by, she said, "Let's get a closer look at this beautiful boat." We walked around, touching the glossy finish of the hand rails. We were so taken by its beauty that we decided to step inside. While we were examining the inside of the boat, suddenly we realized that it had set adrift. We suddenly found ourselves out in the middle of the ocean.

Neither of us knew a thing about steering a boat, so I looked for a radio. I found a compass and lots of switches near the steering wheel. I began to flip the switches, saying, "Mayday! Mayday! Help! We are lost in the middle of the ocean." A voice came over the speaker: "It's okay. I hear you. I will help you. Do you see the compass?"

"Yes," I answered.

The voice said, "Turn the steering wheel until the arrow points directly east. It has to be exactly on the E, not one point to the right or left." I did as he asked. He then said, "You'll be okay. You'll see the lights of the city. You must keep the arrow pointed directly east – don't let it drift one degree to the right or left."

Mother and I carefully watched the silver and black compass, being absolutely sure to keep the needle pointed directly east. It took our full concentration. Finally, our dedication paid off – we saw the lights and then as we got closer we saw family members waiting and cheering as we reached the shore.

We succeeded only by controlling our ship with absolute concentration and care to stay on course to our ultimate destination. In our life journey, we must exercise the same degree of control over our tongues if we are to fulfill our abilities in life, if we are to find the purpose and meaning and goals that we seek. Too often, we overlook how important our words are. Through our words, we share ourselves with the world. When others hear our words, they come to know our personalities, our thoughts, our inner selves.

There are four simple secrets to learning to control our tongues:

The first secret is to allow Christ to search our hearts to help us get rid of any sin that may be lurking there. If there is unrighteousness in our hearts, it will flow out of our mouths. Christ's redeeming power is like a medicine that can heal us.

The second secret is to learn to love others, not just family and friends but all people. When we feel an immense love for other people in our hearts, we exhibit grace to everyone we speak to or about. You can fill your heart with this love by reaching out to our heavenly Father.

Third, we must repent. By repenting, we cleanse our souls and we make the decisions to turn away from our old ways and habits. Begin by asking God to reveal to you the things in your life that are keeping you from becoming all that He created you to be.

Fourth, we need to offer ourselves as a living sacrifice to God, giving ourselves over to His service. I heard a story of a church service in which the pastor spoke about sacrifice. The pastor told the congregation to make a sacrifice to God by laying on the altar anything that was holding them back from completely serving God. One man walked from the back of the church to the altar, knelt down, opened his mouth, and put his tongue on the altar. When I asked later why he had done this, the man responded, "I can't seem to control what I say so I am offering my tongue as a sacrifice to God. I really need His help!"

The more hurting the words we say, the more the words last forever in the minds of the people we speak to. I have heard people say, "I'll forgive, but I won't forget." The words we say can determine a person's self-esteem, their attitude, their performance and even their destiny. What we say does have eternal ramifications. Our speech can be a blessing or a curse to others. Ultimately our speech should be used to draw others closer to God, help them trust Him, to encourage the discouraged, comfort those that mourn and bring joy to the depressed.

Have you ever spoken hurtful words that you regret? Often we hurt most the very ones we love the most.

A woman once went to her pastor asking for help. She had been gossiping about the misdeeds that another woman in the church had allegedly committed. The woman told the pastor that at the time she had gossiped, she had thought everything she was saying was true, although she couldn't remember where she had originally heard the information. Then, to her horror, she had discovered that the rumors were false, and she had tried to apologize, but the lady would not return her telephone calls. What was she to do?

The pastor gave her an assignment. She was to go home, get a feather pillow, and bring it back to his office the next day. Even though this sounded strange, she complied. Before she could speak, the pastor said, "I know you have many questions, and I will answer them in just a minute. But first, cut open the pillow, go to the window, and shake all the feathers outside."

She watched all the feathers blowing in the wind and then returned to her seat. Looking expectantly at the pastor she asked, "Now what, Pastor?"

He responded by saying, "Now, I want you to go outside and collect every one of those feathers. Wherever they are, find each and every one of them and bring them back to me."

Bewildered she stood up and came to the pastor's desk, "But Pastor that is impossible."

He responded by saying calmly, "Yes I know. Just like the words you said about your church friend. They cannot be retrieved. You can't take them back."

Chapter 7

The Power of Touch

One day a thin young man in his 20s came into our offices at Angelic Ministries. As I watched him walk down the hallway, I noticed how unkempt he looked. His clothes were dirty, and the scent of body odor was overwhelming.

I personally took him back to our clothes closet and helped him pick out some clean clothes.

On the way back to the front office, I asked if he needed anything else, and he said he could use some food. As I helped him load up a small box of food, I asked him about his life. He explained that he was living in his car and was looking for work. He had a hardened attitude, and though I shared with him about letting Jesus Christ be Lord of His life, I didn't feel that I had reached through to him. After we had gathered all that he said he needed, we walked toward the door. One of the other staff members came up to us, handing him a Bible to take with him. The three of us were standing there in a circle, and so I asked him if we could say a prayer for him before he left. As I took hold of one of his hands and the other staff member took hold of his other hand, the young man burst into tears almost the minute he felt our touch. "I didn't think anyone cared anymore," he struggled to say in between his sobs.

The power of touch is easy to underestimate.

Touching other human beings and being touched by them in return is more of a necessity than you might think. In Germany, the Hitler regime conducted an inhumane study at one of the concentration camps. Infants were sorted into two groups, and one group was cared for, cuddled, and fed in the arms of nurses. The others in the second group were never held or spoken to; they were given their bottles propped up in their cribs. The end result was not a surprise. Most of the infants who were not touched died while the other ones thrived.

This should speak volumes to all of us concerning the importance of touch in our lives. We should be willing to touch others and be willing to receive it.

The skin is the largest organ of the body and could be described as the wrapping on a package. By looking at someone's skin, we can tell many things about them; how old they are; how they think about themselves; how well they take care of themselves; whether they are sick or healthy.

The book of Matthew tells of an event that happened to Jesus on a busy street.

A man had already come to Jesus pleading with Him to come to his house because his daughter had just died. Jesus was going to this man's house when a woman reached out to touch Him. The woman well knew the importance of touch. She had been suffering from a blood disorder for 12 years and had heard about the healing power of Jesus. She pushed into the crowd, with probably much pain and fear of embarrassment due to her condition, but with a determination to touch Jesus.

The scripture tells us of her great faith: "For she said to herself, 'If only I may touch His garment, so I shall be made well'" (Matthew 9:21). She had so much faith that she believed that just by touching His clothing she would be healed. And the woman was indeed healed that very hour. She understood the importance of a touch. In something as small as a touch, she received so much in return – total healing.

This story is an example of a good touch. Other good touches include a hug, a kiss, a caress, a pat on the back, or stroking someone's hair. All these make the receiver feel special and loved. But sadly in today's world there are many examples of inappropriate touches, a slap, a hit, a punch, even rape and sexual molestation. All of these are unkind and cruel. In order to keep ourselves free from sin, it is our job to make sure that we do not exhibit these types of touches.

The Bible tells us in Romans 6:12-13, "Therefore, do not let sin reign in your mortal body, that you should obey it in its lusts. And do not present your members as instruments of unrighteousness to sin, but present yourselves to God as being alive from the dead, and your members as instruments of righteousness to God."

Society gives mixed messages to all of us. One message we are bombarded with is "if it feels good, do it." This mindset encourages people to care little for others and instead to focus on instant gratification at any cost. As the scripture tells us, we are not to yield any part of our body over to sin. This means all parts of our body and all our senses. Whatever we do, in word or deed or touch, we are to do it in the name of Jesus, giving thanks to God. Our touch should reflect His love in our character.

One of my favorite Bible verses is the description of the love we should strive to have for others. If people everywhere would inscribe these words in their hearts, think what a different world it would be: "Love is patient, love is kind. It does not envy, it does not boast, it is not proud. It is not rude, it is not self-seeking, it is not easily angered, and it keeps no record of wrongs. Love does not delight in evil but rejoices with the truth. It always protects, always trusts, always hopes, always perseveres" (I Corinthians 13:4-7).

If we all lived by these words, there would be no reason to fear inappropriate touches because they would not exist. We will never be as perfect as Jesus Christ on this earth, but we are to strive toward being the best we can be, and learning to love our fellow man is the first step.

The term "learning to love" is used because sometimes we have to learn how to love the unlovable. It is not always easy to give a hug to someone you are angry with, or to shake the hand of someone who is your adversary, but that is what we are called to do. God knew this so He has enabled us to love, by sending His son, Jesus Christ, and our comforter, the Holy Spirit. When a person is saved, Jesus Christ lives inside of him or her, and the love that is expressed through that person is from Jesus Himself. We are a vessel, an earthen vessel, used by God to deliver His message of love, by our words or our deeds, which includes our touch.

The beauty of a butterfly cannot be seen until the cocoon is broken and the insect is released. A flower cannot grow unless the seed that contains it breaks open, setting it free. We, once we have invited Christ to live inside our hearts, must allow His love to be released in our lives. We must avoid keeping Him bottled up. To make a change in others, as well as in ourselves, we all must go through a "breaking" of our sin. This breaking of ourselves is an opening which allows His love to be expressed through our touch to others, and it also allows us to be touched, too, by letting their love reach into ourselves.

When the woman with the blood disorder touched Jesus, the Bible says that at once He realized that power had gone out of him, and He looked around to see who had touched Him. The crowd kept pressing in, and the man whose daughter had just passed was anxious for Jesus to hurry to see His daughter, but Jesus was not in a hurry. It says He kept looking to see who had touched His clothing. Finally the woman came and fell at His feet and explained what had happened.

At that time, Jesus told her, "Daughter, your faith has healed you. Go in peace and be free from your suffering" (Mark 5:32).

Are you determined to reach out toward Jesus Christ as your Savior to receive His blessings for your life? Are you secure in the fact that God lives in you and that His love is yearning to break out toward other people? Is your faith strong enough to battle all odds to express his love to others?

Chapter 8

Guarding Your Senses with the Armor of God

When I was about 13 years old, and just beginning to get interested in boys, my school class took a field trip to a skating rink. On the bus ride there and back, I sat in the third seat from the front with my dearest girlfriend.

A few days after the trip, I was horrified to hear from several students that a teacher at the school was saying that I had sat in the back of the bus with a boy and let him get overly intimate with me. This was back in the 1950s, when a girl's reputation could be permanently ruined by such a rumor. I was doubly hurt that a teacher – someone I respected – was behind the malicious rumor. And I was puzzled – this particular teacher had not even ridden on the same bus as me.

Shaking and crying, I went to my mother with the disgusting tale. She immediately got hold of the teacher's home telephone number and made me call the teacher to sort the situation out. Trembling, my heart pounding, I dialed the number. When the teacher answered, I told her who I was, and I told her about the rumor I had heard. I explained that I had sat on the bus with my girlfriend and suggested that she could ask any number of witnesses who rode on the same bus as to the truth of the matter. The teacher immediately apologized, and asked to speak to my mother, whom she also apologized to. Apparently, the following day she put an end to the rumor at the school, for I never heard any more about it.

I leaned an important lesson from my mother that day. Though I dreaded confronting the teacher over the rumor, my mother made me. She knew that the rumor would grow, and worsen, if not confronted, and she knew that Satan has to be cut off before he can do worse damage.

Just as my mother stood by me that day, encouraging me to do the right (though difficult) thing, so is Christ standing by you to support you as you confront Satan. When you recognize Satan at work, call his hand. If you want to stop Satan dead in his tracks, the key is to learn how to wear the armor of God.

God clearly has prepared armor for us to suit up in. The Bible tells us, "The night is far spent, the day is at hand. Therefore let us cast off the works of darkness, and let us put on the armor of light. Let us walk properly, as in the day, not in revelry and drunkenness, not in lewdness and lust, not in strife and envy. But put on the Lord Jesus Christ, and make no provision for the flesh, to fulfill its lusts" (Romans 13:12-14).

No matter how long we live, where we live, or in what manner we live, we all will experience adversity in our lives. Satan relentlessly does his best to kill all of us through many means, but specifically by entering our senses. Just as the generals and weapon experts make adjustments to their weaponry as their fights progress, so, too, must we be armed with the right gear for the right battles. God has provided equipment for us to use. It is at our disposal. We only have to pick it up.

Trials and battles come in many disguises and from all directions. Our job is to evaluate what they are and to use them to our advantage. The eagle uses the billowing winds of the storm to fly at greater heights. He is not deterred by the severity of rain or snow. By knowing which direction the storm blows, he can soar over it and be safe. Likewise, by determining where our attacks are coming from, we can best decide which weapon to use for battle. A true hunter would never think of taking a machine gun to a turkey shoot or a peashooter on an African safari. Having the correct weapon for battle is essential.

What type of weapons do we have at our disposal? The Bible tells us, "For the weapons of our warfare are not carnal but mighty in God for pulling down strongholds" (II Corinthians 10:4).

The weapons God intends for us to use are "mighty in God" for battle. The Lord has endued power and authority to us. So, we have the weapons and the power and authority to use them, but why don't we? The answer is fear. Fear of the battle, fear of losing, fear of ridicule. Fear has many faces. Fear has been defined as:

False
Evidence
Appearing
Real

In order to fight not only the fear in our lives but more importantly the darts Satan throws at us, we must have faith:

Forsaking
All
I
Trust
Him

"For whatever is not from faith is sin" (Romans 14:23b).

Here is what the Bible tells us about our spiritual armor: Finally, be strong in the Lord and in his mighty power. Put on the full armor of God so that you can take your stand against the devil's schemes. For our struggle is not against flesh and blood, but against the rulers, against the authorities, against the powers of this dark world and against the spiritual forces of evil in the heavenly realms. Therefore put on the full armor of God, so that when the day of evil comes, you may be able to stand your ground, and after you have done everything, to stand. Stand firm then, with the belt of truth buckled around your waist, with the breastplate of righteousness in place, 15and with your feet fitted with the readiness that comes from the gospel of peace. In addition to all this, take up the shield of faith, with which you can extinguish all the flaming arrows of the evil one. Take the helmet of salvation and the sword of the Spirit, which is the word of God. And pray in the Spirit on all occasions with all kinds of prayers and requests. With this is mind, be alert and always keep on praying for all the saints. (Ephesians 6:10-18).

Here is our spiritual armor that God has provided for our offense as well as our defense:

Your sword: the Word of God (1st offensive weapon)
Your intercession: prayer and supplication (2nd offensive weapon)
Your helmet: salvation (1st line of defense)
Your shield: faith (2nd line of defense)
Your breastplate: righteousness (3rd line of defense)
Your loins girded: truth and honesty (4th line of defense)
Your foot armor: the gospel of peace through witnessing (3rd offensive weapon)

As you may have noticed, no part of this armor would cover one's backside. This means two things: God does not want us to be fearful and run from our enemy. He has planned for us to be bold and stand firm, facing forward. It also means that God will be at our back, standing with us with His protection.

Every football game has offensive plays and defensive plays. Offense is when a team has the ball and is basically "attacking" the other team in order to score a touchdown. They have confidence in the fact that they have the ball and have the ability to score if they reach their goal. The other team, on the other hand, is playing the defensive. These players are protecting the goal, guarding it, trying to keep the offensive players from reaching their goal.

In relation to our spiritual armor, God has provided offensive and defensive weapons depending on the various situations and circumstances of the battles. The offense weapons include the Sword of the Spirit (the Bible) and prayer or intercession. When Jesus was taken to the desert for 40 days, Satan tempted him. In order to fight him, Jesus quoted the Word of God back to him and also prayed. We, as Christians, as in the football game, have the possession of the ball (our salvation in Christ) so we should have the confidence to advance on Satan with both barrels.

The weapons of defense are used to defend our position, to protect, and most importantly, to guard our senses.

Helmet of Salvation: By knowing that we accept Christ as our Savior, Lord, and King and that we belong to Him, our faith rests in Him. The result of this faith is courage to fight.

Shield of Faith: This weapon is used when we have a trust centered on God to provide for us and to enable us in battle.

Breastplate of Righteousness: By living in a right manner, by striving to live according to God's plan and direction, we have an inner strength which enables us to turn from temptation.

Loins Girded with Truth: Honesty is a virtue not seen very often in today's society. With slick salesmen, false advertising, and the spin of politicians, whom do we believe? We are to believe in the truth of God. When the author of lies (Satan) throws these darts at us all we have to do is throw the truth back in his face and he will flee. Shod your feet with the gospel of peace. When was the last time you witnessed to a friend or co-worker about the mighty work of God in your life? By sharing with others, not only your faith is upheld but also their faith is built up. I call this a double blessing: when you are blessed, and you share with others what has happened to you, they, too, are blessed by hearing your testimony.

Just as having the correct weapon was helpful for the armies in the Civil War; our weapons have been specifically designed, prepared, and manufactured by God Himself for our use. They have power, if only used. Many Christians are weak in battles because these weapons are lying at their feet. A shield will not protect unless it is held. A helmet will not protect the head if it is not worn. A breastplate will not protect the heart if not put on.

At the beginning of each one of the chapter headings in this book is a Roman soldier, dressed in full armor, ready for battle. This is a picture reminding us that if our senses are to be protected from the world, then our spiritual armor must be worn, shined up, and secure. It is my hope for you that after reading this book you will be fully dressed and ready for battle.

I'd like to leave you with one last encouragement. Though the path to learning to guard your senses can be difficult at first, it does get easier.

When I turned 16, my daddy took me into a field in the country to teach me how to drive his little four-speed white Renault. After showing me several times how to shift the gears, he left me at it while he went back to his work. I bucked that little Renault all over that field, loving the sense of independence and freedom that I got from being able to manipulate the car all alone. I finally caught on to the secret – let the clutch out slowly while giving the engine a little gas. After a few more days of my practicing in the field, daddy took me out on a blacktop highway. He told me that each time I drove, it would get easier. But no matter how expert I might get at it, he cautioned me to always drive defensively.

"Be ready at all times for the unexpected," he warned. "Always focus ahead to see what's coming."

His driving lesson has been one that I've applied to all of life. Making the right choices, putting Christ at the center of your life, guarding your senses – it is all hard work at first, but the more you do it, the easier it becomes. Yet no matter how easy it becomes or how good you get at it, don't let your guard down. Keep your armor on, stay focused on Jesus

Christ, and always look ahead to guard your senses from whatever is coming next.

Appendix I

Prayer of Salvation

Father God, I understand that I am a sinner. I don't want to be alone anymore, trying to live my own life away from You. I know that You love me and want to be my Savior and the Lord of my life. I want that very much. I believe that Jesus Christ, Your Son, died on the cross for my sins, and that to deliver me from the curse of this world He rose in three days to be resurrected.

Please Lord, come into my life and change me. I repent of my sins and turn from them. I open myself up to You to direct my life. Help me to know Your will and to walk in it. Let me be bold in my speech to tell other people of your love and the changes you have made in my life. I love you, Lord.

In Jesus' name I pray,
Amen.

Prayer of Renewal

Lord, I messed up again. I keep trying to follow you but it seems that my will always gets in the way. I recommit my life to you, Father. I don't want you to look down on me and say, "Depart from me, I never knew you." I want you to be able to call me "your good servant."

Lord, I open my life to you, to be directed through the wonderful power of the Holy Spirit. Renew in me the joy of my salvation! I know that You began a good work in me before and have not given up but will complete it. I pray that I may walk worthy of You, Lord, and be pleasing to You in all I do. I pray that I will be fruitful in every good work and continue to increase in the knowledge of who You are; that I will be strengthened with all might through Your power.

For all these things I am grateful and thankful to You for Your Son, Jesus, who died for all my sins. Thank you for not giving up on me and for loving me as your child.

In Jesus' name I pray,
Amen.

Appendix II

About Angelic Ministries

Angelic Ministries opened its doors in downtown Knoxville, Tennessee, in May 2002 with the specific goal of serving families in crisis as well as abused women, homeless men, and children in need. The ministry provides food, clothing, furniture, kitchen utensils, shoes, household items, cars and even homes in some cases.

All of these items come to us by donations. Some donors provide financial support while others donate items. All funding is from private donors or churches. We do not rely on grants or government funding.

Angelic Ministries is grateful to the many churches that have provided support along the way:

- Grace Baptist Church, Knoxville, Tennessee
- Fellowship Evangel
- Cedar Springs
- 2nd Baptist Church
- New Life Methodist
- Cokesbury United Methodist Church
- Church of Christ, Farragut, Tennessee
- Park West Baptist Church
- Fire on the Rock Pentecostal Church
- Heaven Sent Homes for the Hurting

- Lost Sheep Ministries
- Grace Lutheran
- And many others.

As of June 2005, Angelic Ministries has served over 5,000 families, some with as many as 11 children in a single family. By the grace of God, we have been able to supply them with food, linens, furniture, and clothing. In special cases, Angelic Ministries has provided used cars and temporary housing while homeless families and single adults turn their lives around. Most importantly, we offer the services of counseling at no cost, and to all we offer spiritual nurturing with open arms. We also provide hair cuts, training in office work, and music lessons.

Every day we come in contact with hurting people, some whom we forge long-term relationships with and others we see only once. We pray that we will be everything God created us to be to that person in need.

Share with us in our goal to bring more people to know the wonders and power of Jesus Christ: our challenge to you is for you to look for ways to share Christ with others on a daily basis. There are so many ways to be a part of Angelic. Whether it be:

- One hour or 40 hours per week.
- A phone call or word of encouragement.
- Cooking for 20 or 150.
- Serving the food with a smile.
- Committing to praying for Angelic regularly.
- Donating items that can be used by another family.
- Sponsoring one of our people as they go through a year of mentoring and training ($2,500 which includes housing).

This is God's mission field. As people receive they are told about Jesus Christ and His love for them. We see many come to know Him as their Lord and Savior. God needs you. We need you. This is your mission. Pray about how God wants you to be involved here.

Oh, that we may hear Him say, "*Well done, my good and faithful servant*" when we stand before Him.

On Guard

by Betsy Stowers Frazier

I am on guard
In charge of a holy place
I will seek wise council
And look to my Master's face.

I am on guard
A servant as well
Following instructions
His story to tell

I am on guard
Twenty-four hours a day
Security is essential
No time to play

I am on guard
And the end draws near
I will not allow
Satan to enter here

Be Careful Little Eyes

The following is a song I learned to sing as a child. I have found that these words hold truth for us as adults today.

Be careful little eyes what you see
Be careful little eyes what you see
For the Father up above
Is looking down in love
Oh, be careful little eyes what you see

Be careful little ears what you hear
Be careful little ears what you hear
For the Father up above
Is looking down in love
Oh, be careful little ears what you hear

Be careful little feet where you go
Be careful little feet where you go
For the Father up above
Is looking down in love
Oh, be careful little feet where you go.

My Father's House

by Betsy Stowers Frazier

I am my Father's house
For He lives in me, you see
I am my Father's house
He loves hanging out with me

I am my Father's house
And he left me in charge today
I am my Father's house
I'll take care while He's away.

Appendix III

Scripture Helps

Sense of Sight

Luke 11: 34-35
Your eye is the lamp of your body. When your eyes are good, your whole body also is full of light. But when they are bad, your body also is full of darkness. See to it, then, that the light within you is not darkness.

I John 2:15-17
Do not love the world or the things in the world. If anyone loves the world, the love of the Father is not in him. For all that is in the world – the lust of the flesh, the lust of the eyes, and the pride of life – is not of the Father but is of the world. And the world is passing away, and the lust of it; but he who does the will of God abides forever.

II Corinthians 4:3-4
And even if our gospel is veiled, it is veiled to those who are perishing. The god of this age has blinded the minds of unbelievers, so that they cannot see the light of the gospel of the glory of Christ, who is the image of God.

II Corinthians 4:18
We fix our eyes not on what is seen but on what is unseen. For the things which are seen are temporary, but the things which are not seen are eternal.

II Corinthians 8:21
For we are taking pains to do what is right, not only in the eyes of the Lord, but also in the eyes of men.

II Corinthians 10:3-5
For though we live in the world, we do not wage war as the world does. The weapons we fight with are not the weapons of the world. On the contrary, they have divine powers to demolish strongholds.

James 4:14, 17
Whereas you do not know what will happen tomorrow. For what is your life? It is even a vapor that appears for a little time and then vanishes away. Therefore to him who knows to go do well and does not do it, to him it is sin.

Galatians 5:16
So I say live by the Spirit, and you will not gratify the desires of the sinful nature.

Sense of Hearing

John 5:24
Most assuredly, I say to you, he who hears my word and believes in Him who sent me has everlasting life, and shall not come into judgment, but has passed from death into life.

Ephesians 5:6
Let no one deceive you with empty words, for because of these things the wrath of God comes upon the sons of disobedience.

James 1:19
My dear brothers, take note of this: Everyone should be quick to listen, slow to speak and slow to become angry.

John 8:47
He who belongs to God hears what God says. The reason you do not hear is that you do not belong to God.

Psalm 34:17
The righteous cry out, and the Lord hears them; He delivers them from all their troubles.

James 1:22
Do not merely listen to the word and so deceive yourself. Do what it says.

II Timothy 4:3-4
For the time will come when men will not put up with sound doctrine. Instead, to suit their own desires, they will gather around them a great number of teachers to say what their itching ears want to hear. They will turn their ears away from the truth and turn aside to myths.

Romans 10:13-14
For whosoever shall call upon the name of the Lord shall be saved. How then shall they call on him in whom they have not believed? And how shall they believe in him of whom they have not heard? And how shall they hear without a preacher?

Sense of Smell

Psalm 115:2-8
Why do the nations say, "Where is their God?" Our God is in heaven; he does whatever pleases him. But their idols are silver and gold, made by hands of men. They have mouths, but cannot speak, eyes, but cannot see; they have ears but cannot hear; noses, but they cannot smell; they have hands, but cannot feel, feet but they cannot walk; nor can they utter a sound with their throats. Those who make them will be like them and so will all who trust in them.

II Corinthians 2:15-16
For we are to God the aroma of Christ among those who are being saved and those who are perishing. To the one we are the smell of death; to the other, the fragrance of life. And who is equal to such a task?

Hebrews 5:13-14
For every one that uses milk is unskillful in the word of righteousness; for he is a babe. But strong meat belongs to them that are of full age, even those who by reason of use have their senses exercised to discern both good and evil.

Sense of Taste

Matthew 12:37
For by your words you will be acquitted, and by your words you will be condemned.

Ephesians 4:29-30
Let no corrupt word proceed out of your mouth, but what is good for necessary edification, that it may impart grace to the hearers. And do not grieve the Holy Spirit of God by whom you were sealed for the day of redemption.

Ephesians 5:3-5 K.J.
But fornication and all uncleanness or covetousness, let it not even be named among you, as if fitting for saints; neither filthiness, nor foolish talking, nor coarse jesting, which are not fitting, but rather giving of thanks. For this you know, that no fornicator, unclean person, nor covetous man, who is an idolater, has any inheritance in the kingdom of Christ and God.

James 3:5-8 K.J.
Even so the tongue is a little member and boasts great things. See how great a forest a little fire kindles. And the tongue is a fire, a world of iniquity. The tongue is so set among our members that it defiles the whole body, and sets on fire the course of nature; and it is set on fire by hell. For every kind of beast and bird, of reptile and creature of the sea, is tamed and has been tamed by mankind. But no man can tame the tongue. It is an unruly evil, full of deadly poison.

James 3:9-12
With it (the tongue) we bless our God and Father, and with it we curse men, who have been made in the similitude of God. Out of the same mouth proceed blessings and cursing. My brethren, these things ought not to be so. Does a spring send forth fresh water and bitter from the same opening? Can a fig tree, my brethren, bear olives, or a grapevine bear figs? Thus no spring yields both salt water and fresh.

I Thessalonians 5:21, 22
Test all things, hold fast what is good; abstain from every form of evil.

Proverbs 16:23, 24
The heart of the wise teaches his mouth. And addeth learning to his lips. Pleasant words are like a honeycomb. Sweetness to the soul and health to the bones.

Proverb s 16:27-28
An ungodly man digs up evil, and it is on his lips like a burning fire. A perverse man sows strife, and a whisperer separates the best of friends.

Proverbs 17:4
An evildoer gives heed to false lips; a liar listens eagerly to a spiteful tongue.

Sense of Touch

II Timothy 2:22-23
Flee also youthful lusts; but pursue righteousness, faith, love, peace with those who call on the Lord out of a pure heart. But avoid foolish and ignorant disputes, knowing that they generate strife.

Galatians 5:16-26
I say then: Walk in the Spirit, and you shall not fulfill the lusts of the flesh. For the flesh lusts against the Spirit and the Spirit against the flesh; and these are contrary to one another, so that you do not do the things you wish. But if you are led by the Spirit you are not under the law. Now the works of the flesh are evident, which are adultery, fornication, uncleanness, lewdness, idolatry, sorcery, hatred, contentions, jealousies, outbursts of wrath, selfish ambitions, dissensions, heresies, envy, murders, drunkenness, revelries, and the like; of which I tell you beforehand. Just as I also told you in time past, that those who practice such things will not inherit the kingdom of God. But the fruit of the Spirit is love, joy, peace, longsuffering, kindness, goodness, faithfulness, gentleness, self-control. Against such there is no law. And those who are Christ's have crucified the flesh with its passions and desires. If we live by the Spirit let us also walk in the Spirit.

Romans 6:13
And do not present your members as instruments of unrighteousness to sin, but present yourselves to God as being alive from the dead, and your members as instruments of righteousness to God.

I Corinthians 15:33
Do not be deceived. Evil company corrupts good behavior.

II Corinthians 6:17, 19
Therefore come out from among them and be separate, says the Lord. Do not touch what is unclean, and I will receive you.

II Corinthians 7:1
Therefore, having these promises, beloved, let us cleanse ourselves from all filthiness of the flesh and spirit, perfecting holiness in the fear of God.

I Corinthians 3:16, 17
Do you not know that you are the temple of God and that the Spirit of God dwells in you? If anyone defiles the temple of God, God will destroy him. For the temple of God is holy, which temple you are?

LaVergne, TN USA
10 January 2010
169487LV00002B/2/P